HE WESLEYAN POETRY PROGRAM

"What we are out to do in The Wesleyan Poetry Program is not necessarily to discover new talent, or to rediscover neglected talent, or to encourage the experimental— though these and other motives have swayed us from time to time; our purpose and satisfaction lie in giving book publication to fine poetry of whatever sort, in a period when American publishing as a whole still hesitates to do justice to the art."

—RICHARD WILBUR

Manuscripts for consideration are welcomed from anyone. There are no restrictions of form or of style. They are read by the three members of the especial editorial board that makes publishing recommendations, distinguished poets and critics, whose single criterion of acceptance is excellence.

At least four volumes are published each year, two or more in the spring and two or more in the fall. Each book is issued simultaneously in clothbound and paperbound editions.

"The most exciting poetry program in current American publishing."

—*The Sewanee Review*

"Any library collection concerned with the life of poetry beyond mid-century should include the remarkable volumes of The Wesleyan Poetry Program."

—*Choice*

The Poets of The Wesleyan Poetry Program

Alan Ansen, John Ashbery, Robert Bagg, Michael Benedikt, Robert Bly, Gray Burr, Turner Cassity, Evans Chigounis, Tram Combs, Donald Davie, James Dickey, William Dickey, Russell Edson, D. J. Enright, David Ferry, Calvin Forbes, Robert Francis, Cynthia Genser, Dugan Gilman, Barbara L. Greenberg, John Haines, Kenneth O. Hanson, William Harmon, Judith Hemschemeyer, Edwin Honig, Richard Howard, Barbara Howes, David Ignatow, Donald Justice, Chester Kallman, Dave Kelly, Adam LeFevre, Eleanor Lerman, Charles Levendosky, Philip Levine, Lou Lipsitz, Clarence Major, Josephine Miles, Vassar Miller, W. R. Moses, Leonard Nathan, James Nolan, Steve Orlen, Donald Petersen, Marge Piercy, Hyman Plutzik, David Ray, Vern Rutsala, James Seay, Harvey Shapiro, Jon Silkin, Louis Simpson, Anne Stevenson, Stephen Tapscott, James Tate, Richard Tillinghast, Frederick Turner, Ellen Bryant Voigt, Shirley Williams, Charles Wright, James Wright

EVERYTHING ALL AT ONCE

The Wesleyan Poetry Program: Volume 89

EVERYTHING
ALL AT ONCE

POEMS

BY ADAM LEFEVRE

WESLEYAN UNIVERSITY PRESS

MIDDLETOWN, CONNECTICUT

Grateful acknowledgment is made to the following magazines, in which some of these poems have appeared: *The Nation, The Paris Review, Arion's Dolphin, Pique,* and *The River City Companion.*

The publisher gratefully acknowledges the support of the publication of this book by the Andrew W. Mellon Foundation.

Library of Congress Cataloging in Publication Data

LeFevre, Adam, 1950–
      Everything all at once.

      (Wesleyan poetry program; v. 89)
      I. Title.
PS3562.E374E9   811'.5'4   77-14847
ISBN 0-8195-2089-6
ISBN 0-8195-1089-0 pbk.

Manufactured in the United States of America
First edition

to my mother and my father

✳✳

CONTENTS

EVERYTHING ALL AT ONCE

The Autopsy

It was up to the doctors.

They unzipped the dead man
and discovered sleeping, made out of coal.
They unzipped the sleeping
and discovered windows made of distance.
They unzipped the windows
and discovered an oriole, also dead.
They unzipped the oriole
and discovered what they thought were human tears,
    but chemical analysis proved it was sea water.
They unzipped the sea water
and discovered footprints.
They unzipped the footprints
and discovered more footprints,
    which continued until the wee hours of the morning,
    when the doctors unzipped the footprints
and discovered a deep sky,
    which they immediately concluded
    was the cause of death.

Ethics

Where I went to college in the purple valley of northwest Massachusetts, there was a fellow in my class who used to drag a brick around by a string. He called it his "pet brick." Every night he would drag his brick into the campus snack bar when the snack bar was most crowded, and order two vanilla milkshakes—one for himself, one for his brick. The first time I saw him I laughed at the absurdity of the proposition. A pet brick! A brick drinking a milkshake! The subsequent occasions of my seeing this fellow and his brick made me respond differently. Often I was angry, thinking he dragged the brick for just the clamor that will always attend the outrageous. Sometimes, when I could convince myself that he and his brick were actually a charade protesting technology gone wild or man's inhumanity to man, I could feel the pleasant twinge of belonging to a fraternity of hoodwinkers. But when I saw him in the early morning, dragging his brick through the empty quad, my heart would fill with the silent despair that rose from the strange interplay between them. Just as it was impossible to know exactly how he felt about the brick, in those days I never knew how I should feel about anything. Only one thing was clear. He did not love the brick. Nor did the brick love him. This fact became my reference point in all matters of faith.

Listen

Don't the dead love you?
Don't they understand every poem
you write them, even
the most ambiguous?

Still you try to remember
something else.
You sunbathe. You eat.
(Habits that disgust them,
but do they say one word?)

And don't you go days
without giving them one
thought, and don't they woo
you constantly with silence,
perfectly discreet?

Still you make them
the butt of your cruelest jokes.
And you lie to them. You lie
through your teeth.
You think they're ugly.
You should say so.

They won't throw a tantrum.
They're happy just to hear
you breathe.
That's how much they love you.

Facts About Nature 1

Ants do not eat fingers.

In South America there are ants
    the size of your hand.

They grow that way
    because of the warm, moist climate.

If you are walking in the rain
    forests down in South America,
you will walk under giant umbrella trees
beneath which fingers
    are neatly piled.

That means the ants have been there.

Another Poem About Poetry

Wherever I go,
I carry two leather suitcases
full of mud. Understand,
I'm not a religious man.
The idea of meeting my maker
disgusts me.

I admire the articulate screw
that patterns itself
on the circular declensions
of buzzards.

I say, so what if there is no soldier
in the Tomb of the Unknown Soldier.

Hurrah for the sluttishness of objects!

Often in my dreams I have risen
against my will, crashing through the trees
and clouds, into the blue saliva.

No wonder I envy the worm's one sense.

No wonder the non-edible is meaningless to me.

I hope my behavior does not offend.
Understand, even the distance between us
can be folded to fit in my mouth.
Understand, you are very edible, so far
as I'm concerned.

The Hunter

The hunter leans into the mountain. He is sorry for the bacon. He is sorry for the eggs and the blueberry muffins he ate before dawn. Now he has to take a terrible shit. He looks around.

The mountainside is jagged and steep. But the trees have roots, the sky, incredible tenacity. Nature crows, "I'm adequate." But he can find no place to shit in it. There is scrub all around, and where there is no scrub, there is an impossible pitch. So he keeps climbing, the pain in his bowels growing every step. *I am going to die,* he thinks.

Then he sees a boulder, flat on top, stuck like a tick in the mountainside. Actually, a glacier rammed it in there about a million years ago. But the hunter doesn't care where it came from. He leans his rifle against it, clambers to the top, scraping his fingers on the lichen. There is a fault in the rock.

A cleft. A fissure. *Perfect,* he thinks. He drops his pants and squats, straddling the fault like a rugged philosophy. The rough red wool of his mackinaw prickles on his penis, and the cold wind pries his ass.

When the hunter shits, his sorrow falls deep into the rock. Once again he can love being among the animals. Once again he can climb breathless to hang their faces on his wall.

Sestina Sestina

The sestina is a difficult form
to master because of the excessive repetition
which usually seems gratuitous or else
makes the speaking voice sound downright mad.
Psychologists say madness characterizes our time.
That may be. For some reason the sestina

is an obsession of mine. My first sestina
was a complete failure. The form
tangled me in a net. By the time
I reached stanza two, the repetition
blabbed like an obnoxious drunk. I got so mad
I swore, and swore I'd write a good sestina or else.

I worked at nothing else,
only the sestina. Day and night, one insipid sestina
after another. Every one I made made me mad.
I should never have strayed from the open forms.
They seem like a fairyland now. Repetition
enchants the mind until time

itself seems to be a sestina. In no time
my universe was bound to six words and nothing else
mattered. That's the danger of repetition.
It creates an illusion of eternity. The sestina
appears to be its own heaven. The form,
fulfilled, has that appeal. So does mad-

ness, psychologists say. But the mad
are their own poems. Their time
is malleable—no need to conform
to architecture designed by someone else.
The maker of sestinas
sulks under the weight of repetition,

flails in a snarl of repetition,
repeating himself like a nervous zodiac for his nomad
mind. So stay away from sestinas.
There are better ways to spend your time.
Write a novel. Take up the guitar. Or else
stifle your creative impulses altogether. Chloroform

the Muse! This form is a hungry monster.
Repetition wants something else every time. Six
mad kings and you, locked in a cell—that's a sestina.

Pickup

She was petite.
No. She was sitting down.
She was blessed with a certain grace
of being, as opposed to real beauty.
Knowing her was like bowling a perfect game.
She was well bred and well
fed. Small boned but hefty.
She carried helplessness with her
like an imaginary suitcase.
She was an accomplished
Red Cross volunteer, an avid seamstress.
She spoke three languages,
each one a little differently.
She was alone in the world,
in a suede jacket with a novel
in her lap. She didn't want to bore you,
so she screwed you to a confession.
She blushed when you mentioned suicide,
but kissed you like a meathook.
Her eyes glowed like cigarettes
in the dark closet of your privacy.
All the time you knew it was wrong, the way
she rubbed you, but you pitched in.
Not what you'd imagined, an out and out *human*,
she beat you with the wings of her desperate
breathing.
Yes, she fit you to her,
this pretender, this dejected angel,
and she wore you well,
all the way down.

Vampire Bride

A bouquet of blue pistons and razor blades
she holds in her hands.
Her dead grandmother's lace gown,
tucked, shortened.
And the veil she made herself
over the years, over her face

like a spider. Again she said yes—always
the hopeless romantic, the archaic maid.
Crouching behind his hearse,
the undertaker undoes the cans.
He, too, saw her naked, and was content
a better man won.

Cold feet is his only explanation.
Look at her, most beautiful in disgrace!
What she must be thinking! Each present
to return, apology made.
Each lie, "a sudden change in plans."
Reverse, and double reverse,

and still she's hers,
with all she disowned:
her breath, the subjunctive errand
of her nights and days,
her golden ring, her afraid
eyes and their reticence.

At last the priest begins to sense
the meaning of love, like a horse
its falling rider. "I'm afraid
I can't marry you," he blurts. The organ,
programmed for any occasion, plays
St. James Infirmary. Relations dance

around the altar. With desperate nonchalance
they toss black rice, in deference
to her hope that when she dies again she stays
dead. She's the source
of all the trouble they have known.
She's the promise they insist they never made.

The Boots of Guilt

some need them
others don't think
they need them but
need them others think the
other guy should have them
if he needs them more than
some others who if they need them
think they need them more than any
others need some need who are the fat
cats and who needs them? I don't
think they don't need something though some
think they do others don't think about it much
they think about their own need which is natural just
imagine if nobody needed anything and like the lone sur-
vivor of a tragic airplane crash you've deified the
haphazard.

Nordic Anthem

Dog your property, from waterline to songbird.
Or the malarial bandit, whose pain for others is god-
     like,
Will he hesitate for eight minutes to make off with
     every last tillika?
Having escaped, won't be boast out loud in the worst
     Viking tradition?

Mind your isolated beaches. Or do you love the
     uxorial ethos
Sucking up Almighty Karlek in its belly dance?
O my electric light! How deep must I bury you
Until I'm safe in the rings of wood?

From the far fort, he and I took off our lumber.
From the far fort, he saw the glimmering spy,
The bone-dry bride in the dragon's den, and thunder,
The dragon, some ingots, the distant licking of
     eaten bird.

The world rhymed in the long run. Far flung hellos
Frisked the distant afterlife like conifers the
     lowlife sky.
To and fro new arrows flew.
I would shout without speaking a name, without
     pleasure of it.

Him! by God! For eight bloody minutes!
And female noise of his inland crew
Rising from the oak stumps!
Did Ingeborg use his father's sword without asking?
O raft full of jewels!
Blood in the quiver of Uncle Pesadore!

Electrocute him, by God! Alone in the sky.
Skin the fatherland without the slightest woman.
Cover the older warbabies with surgical hair,
And offer dug-up meals, gray feminine food.
Vanish and offer land, offer sojourns,
Afternoons to skim the taiga,
An air for burial, sky noise, and dinner.

To fetch the farfetched widow they price, or price
Uncertainty for a motor in God's arcade.
They roar ever boning for Karlek, the hurt demi-god!
They roar ever duty, their sight the reindeer's burden.
They roar prepared meat, their darned skin flapping!
To be seated! To splatter the wooden lake!

Summertime, North Conway,
New Hamsphire

Off-white peasant blouse;
shorts, a sherbet orange;
turtle-rimmed sunglasses riding
her peachy brow, and

sandals made in Mexico delicately
clopping the cobbled walks
and the unfinished floors of the clothing
shops, SNAZ, REAL EARTH; looking

for nothing in particular
because it's vacationtime in the White Mountains
and she's "another person,"
tuned to a low hum, arms

nutbrown, teeth especially
white, her husband
golfing, the entire afternoon
to herself and this

resort, nothing on her mind
but a simple blue scarf
to keep the sun off
in the peasant fashion.

Oh New Hampshire! Frosted
hair so distinguished it's blue!
Oh woman, enthralled by the mountains,
those manikins!

Oh philosophy!
Oh late lunch!
Oh automatic window!

Lullaby for Father

Tit! baby cries.
Day! Day! What can
Father do? As Father,
what can he do?

His breasts are onions.
All he can offer
is opinions.
The nursery is just

one vowel! Oh!
Turn to the dark wind, Father.
Turn to milk, Dark Wind.
Come back, Sun, old bachelor,

back from your whore!

Aubade

A big nun is sitting on an azimuth.
Behind her back, the dark opens like hands
released from prayer
Snakes and rodents crawl out
in every direction.
The eyes of the nun are wet with love.
Between her legs the sun is rising.

Facts About Nature 2

Zero stands for nothing.
But how very important it is to us!
Without zero, our universe would be a vulgar
     proposition indeed.

Zero is all around us,
like the mouth of a choirboy.
Look at your body. How many zeros can you find?

Your bellybutton? Your asshole?
Actually, your whole body may just be
a multitude of zeros, cleverly stacked.

Zero in the sky! Zero in your pocket!
Doesn't the sun look like a zero? Doesn't a penny?
Imagine the eyes of someone you love.

Can you see zeros within zeros?
What about a bullethole? What about a lifesaver? What
     about a whole pie?
Did you ever wonder why a dog turns round

and round before lying down to sleep, like water
going down a drain?
I think it may have something to do with zero.

How many zeros can you find in the word *good?*
How many zeros can you find in this poem about zero?
Do you think it is better to think about zero than
     nothing?

Why do you think this is so?

My Lust

Out of breath,
standing at a crossroads

where no signs are,
and each road looks like the same road—

poor messenger!
when the most sensible thing to do is

become hysterical, turn
in circles, and shout

the message over
and over to each distance.

The Coma

He got up to see why it wasn't light yet, and noticed a downy white mold on the inside of the window. He scrubbed it with antiseptic, and in no time the window regained its transparency. He could see the city once again, so familiar to him with its old-world clocktower, its fussy harbor, its illogical streets and their files of traffic. He spent the rest of the morning secure in the deep pile of metaphysical thought, and was disturbed around lunchtime to discover night had fallen. When he went to the window he saw to his great amazement that it now sported a three-day growth of beard. He stropped his razor and shaved the window, and sure enough, it was just noon on a run-of-the-mill day. He spent the afternoon bent over his note-books, enumerating in neat paragraphs the ramifications of window hair, alluding to Darwin and Dada, making some startling phenomenological pronouncements. By suppertime the window had regrown its black stubble, and he shaved it again, just in time to enjoy a superlative blood-red sunset. That evening he amused himself with cognac and acrostics until very late, until the window's beard hung to the floor—by his calculations, nearly morning.

Theoretical Landscape

When unpredictable areas take over
(as if clouds, the original tumors, could be plucked!),
the known will entice its previous life
with a motherly cunning.
No invisible police, no songstress of sentimental
mistakes like the ability to forget,
nor blending in can swathe that attempt.
Because when metaphor requires metaphor
it's like a ladle lost in hot stew.
Just imagine the power of a misplaced
    decimal point.
Just imagine where anything is all right.

The Difficult Birth of Mr. Walt Disney

One fine morning in a bright green garden an old man sat crying. His white beard wound round him like a friendly serpent. The big sky was so blue, and the little birds singing. The smiling sun cast warm nets over him, as the gentle breeze did blow. The old man looked up. His eyes were so red from crying. *I want! I want!* he cried in his old broken voice.

The birds stopped singing. They swallowed their songs and flew away. The sun frowned and sailed off in its dark cloudboat. The old man sat crying. And the air was so still.

The beautiful flowers jumped down their stems, and the stems darted into the ground. And the trees took back their leaves until the garden was quite brown. Then little white patches appeared on the ground, like a rash that grew. It was the snow! coming back! It flew up, up into the air!

And when the white curtain was up, geese honked in the bones of the sky. There was a baby boy, brilliant and crying in the cold.

Scapulae

Shaped like digging
tools, like spades,
but they have no taste
for earth.

More like ancients
recalling some necessity
too distant from us,
too likely imagined.

They insist they once were wings-
back when men were angels.

Insist.
That's what they do, the blades.
Just under the skin.
More like a mind,
like water underground.

Feel them in back of your love
as you press her to you.
Feel them insisting.
Poor old wings.

The Night Charles Darwin Drank Too Much

Despite the full moon, he couldn't find his way back to the ship. He threw up on the beach. He pulled his shirttail out to wipe the vomit from his lips. "Thank God the men can't see me in this condition," he thought. He was looking out to sea. A wave put a starfish on the beach in front of him, like a penny for his thoughts. "Have you seen my ship the *Beagle?*" asked Darwin. The starfish pointed in five directions until a messiah bird swooped down and ate it. "Bird," said Darwin, "I have lost my ship. Perhaps from the air you have seen it." And the bird said, "Bird-I-have-lost-my-ship-perhaps-from-the-air-you-have-seen-it. Bird-I-have-lost-my-ship-perhaps-from-the-air-you-have-seen it," and flew away. A wave washed over Darwin's shoes. "I have lost my ship," said Darwin. "Have you seen the *Beagle?*" " 'Ask the next wave,' said the wave," said the wave. And Darwin did, on all fours, and the waves carried him out to sea.

Illumination of 1803

Now I am a man.
But then I was a woman,
mistress to Thomas Malthus,
curate of Albury at Surrey.
In the goosedown of his secret bed
he'd labor over me,
and I would bite his ears,
which he liked.
And when he'd come
with a groan like old wood,
my moon, my petunia he'd call me,
though I was a thick farm girl
the color of dusk.
And now I remember the dew
that darkened my skirts as I ran
the meadows from the vicarage,
just as light and the crows
were filling the beechgrove.
And I remember conceiving,
and Master Thomas forswearing.
No more, woman! he said.
Undowered I
was given to the wind,
abandoned with that light
unravelling within me.

Where were you then, my love?
How I cried, hoping
to dislodge your soul like night
from the separate stars.
But you were woven
in another body,
fettered with another
variety of thought.

How I wish you could have
set sail then from America,
arrived and loved me,
Thomas Jefferson!

Western

for Soo

She gets fresh towels and the water boiling.
He spares a bullet for me to bite on.
He's going to wrench the arrow
from my thigh, or shove it through
if he has to.
She's going to help.

I'm all lather. She's
sweating too. He's
not sweating. He's a blacksmith.
She, a haberdasher. Me,
a stranger.
My horse brought me here.

I was canting through a stand of pines.
I was heading east when the missile struck.
That was some Saturdays ago.
My horse brought me here.

She pins my shoulders, for the pain
maddens me.
Easy she says *You're going to be
all right.*
Please help me I say.

I'm going fast.
My horse hawks the news.
The last of the West!
The gen-yoo-ine article!
Snow falls on the Rockies.

But she tends my eyes
with soft brushes
of her fluffy wings!

O thank you I say. And *I'm sorry for what
I done.*
She kisses me, and her face blows away
like tumbleweed.

And it's only my horse, licking my face.
Just steam from his soft black nostrils.

The Love Story with the Ironic, Happy Ending

After she left, I became my own worst enemy. On sunny days, I would punch myself in the eye. When it rained, you could find me perched like a gargoyle on top of the nearest lightning rod. One night during a storm, unscrupulous gypsies, combining a sharp eye for a buck with genuine sympathy for the homeless, lured me down with promises of everlasting death. Instead, they just tied me up with old rope and hung me like some ornamental relief from the side of their lead wagon! In this manner I was displayed at shopping malls and church bazaars as *Griefman*. My tattered suit and vacant gaze brought a tidy sum. Plump mothers would advise their slack-jawed children that I was what would happen if they didn't eat their vegetables. Except for an occasional teenage hoodlum spitting on my toes to impress his giggling sweetheart, this life was not un-pleasant. In fact, I began to relish living as never before. Because my role in the world, so long disguised in the motley of love and hate, was now revealed to me. I was a sensation. People traveled days and paid great sums for just a glimpse of me. And the gypsies kept me with a tenderness usually reserved for the greatest works of art.

Then one day like a bolt from the blue she returned! I spotted her in the afternoon crowd that was filing by. Because of the un-kempt beard which now drooped to my ankles, she would not rec-ognize me—unless I somehow confessed myself to her. Was there ever a second when I was tempted to delude her? No. She was al-ways my true love, and I could not hesitate to inform her. But hard as I tried, I could not remember her name. Hard as I tried, I could not speak at all. Not one word lurked in the alley of my throat. Now she was standing right in front of me! I could see in her eyes my absolute and unrequited joy!

Sequence: Brady at Cold Harbor

Into the orchard
goes Brady
3-legged camera
over his shoulder
like a captured woman.

1, 2, 3, 4 . . .
Brady pacing the distance
from his subject,
a gray corpse,
supine, mouth wide,
as if eating sky.

Brady adjusting the tripod.
How gently he touches his camera!
Notice the lines above his eyes
as he squints
to evaluate the light.

There's Brady
removing his spectacles.

There's Brady,
his head covered
with a black cloth.

1, 2, 3, 4 . . .
Brady in the orchard
counting time out
loud for the light.

Elegy for a Taxidermist

Because death
must mean something,
there is his
wife, locking
the door to his
workroom, just
as he left it:

Hornaday's book, held
to the chapter on
facial expression
by a scalpel
and a jar of powdered
arsenic; the unfinished
head, lying on its side;

and the drawer, half
open, of unused eyes.
On the wall, the calendar,
a woman without clothes,
Miss June, forever June.

Willie Mays

The great-great-great grandfather of Vic Wertz was a Rumanian count. Although Count Wertz's concerns were agrarian in the main, he was also an amateur astronomer. For in that post-Newtonian age, it was necessary to dabble. Hot summer nights he climbed to the turret of Castle Wertz with the lenses he ground himself, and gazed at the heavens. Even then, the quasars ranged outward! Even then, God was in question! Perhaps the thick aroma of bedewed fertility that rose from his asleep wheatfields was all that kept the Count from jumping, one midnight, out into the air, instead of slowly descending the winding stairs, lantern in hand, down to the master bedroom, where his beautiful worried wife sat up reading.

Class Picture

You may find it amusing now
that someone was holding two fingers
like horns behind your head
as you presented yourself to history.

The deadpan of your accuser
and the photographer's honest boredom
both escaped you. Now, expert in tormenting
and contentious dreams, you have learned
to remember perfectly the hilarity
of that day of your death.

Love Takes Heartland

The hairiest body in the whole
high school, but fingers like
white keys. Hunk's sweetie says
Hunk's so kind it makes her cry
when he thumbs her.
Hunk is no meatball!
Maybe in the metal shop,
but by the light of the old Coleman
lantern in Aunt Vi's smokehouse
those close August nights
when his mouth softens
on hers and her face
explained by his hands
becomes the air, Hunk says
Oh Cynthia! and tornadoes
do-si-do over Kansas.

Photograph

The man about to be conceived stands in the rain,
charmed by some mysterious smell—

septic, like spillage, or old wood,
but not actually that.

In a moment he may remember
where he's smelled it before,

and his mood, the exact position
of objects around him, realign.

It would be a sort of miracle.
More likely he'll never remember,

or not until a time when memory alone
is sufficient, when he won't need

what he's thinking now: *like compost,
like semen, like broken glass*

would smell if glass bled . . .

The Lost Astronaut

How long now
    since the retro-
rockets failed he
    cannot know.
Outside the usual
    egg of time
memory floats
    like a drowned angel.

On earth, thank God, we will remember
    conventionally—another day
of no business, no mail;
    dozing in a hammock wondering

how it is *out there,*
    locked in a theoretical present,
born and reborn
    again and again
as his spaceship drifts forever
    away from what he may have meant.

We earthlings must suffer
    in more precise terms.
So we commemorate his profile
    on our change.
We use his name
    in our everyday language
until it takes root there
    and becomes
a name for a name.

The Pheasant Hunter

Diligence in the fallow.
Row by row
the pheasant hunter goes
through the corn stubble.

A Cartesian in a red hat,
looking for the complete experience,
looking for something to take with him.

If there's pheasant in this field
he means to have it.

So he goes and goes, like a reader
line by line,
and the ground gives a little
under his boots
with the crunch of first frost.

Monologue of the Girl in the Refrigerator

To be last.
To find the best place
and stay, like God,
till the end;
reveal oneself only
when everyone confessed
the perfection of the absence.
We all agreed to that
intention.

But I went farther than anyone
away from the counting—
thousand one, thousand two—
nearer the county dump than parents
would permit,
rushing through pin oak, sumac, and speargrass,
till I came to this bin,
this dried up sinkhole, low in a weedfield,
and its creche of abandoned appliances,
toppled washer, rusted mangle,
and an old refrigerator,
plump and empty as a grandmother,
and I climbed out of the air
into this indulging obscurity.

Now I know where heaven is.

My old places,
the crawlspace beneath the porches,
the leafpiles, and the dreamy midst
of Mrs. Romano's unkempt lilac,
i leave for you, my playmates,
to learn and forget,
as for the sad-eyed bloodhounds I left
the scent of my Sunday pumps.

And for the one who will find me,
these directions to heaven—
it's close,
close and dark,
and the door opens
just from your side.

Winter Birds

I'm a thing!
I'm a thing!
All morning long
the birds

in the dead
trees
trill their mindless
certainties.

But intelligence can't express
its gratitude for emptiness.

Villanelle of the Nuclear Physicists

The smallest particle has been split.
We must split it again and again
until the inside is outside of it.

The unknown mocks us—like an egg in a catcher's mitt.
So we make the world explain.
The smallest particle has been split.

We are gutting the Infinite,
that imperious old hen,
until the inside is outside of it,

useless as sex to a ghost. The bottomless pit
does not frighten scientific men.
The smallest particle has been split.

Praise to the sky that keeps its secret
poorly, out of excitement. Let the dark open
until the inside is outside of it,

and heaven is lit
with death and pain.
The smallest particle has been split.
The inside is outside of it.

Facts About Nature 3

Eurydice's Hairpin. Cassandra's Curse.

These are the names of wildflowers
that come out just at night,
in the remotest woods,
during no moon.

You can't hunt them with a flashlight or a match.
They'll get wind of any glimmer and close up
and slip back into the earth.

Even the invisible light of your own eyes
will frighten them.

You have to go on hands and knees, eyes closed
groping delicately with your fingertips.

It's painful.

When you come home
at sunrise, hands bloody, forehead bumped
and blue, the knees of your pants worn through
your loved ones call you "crazy idiot."

But never mind.
They are not your loved ones.
These flowers are.

And when you find them,
when you hold them in your hands
you get one wish, beginning
I don't want.

Two Portraits

I. *Portrait with a Sigh*

He peels an orange
and eats it, spitting
the seeds in the wastebasket.
After fiddling with the radio,
he turns it off.
He enumerates in his head
the principles of the internal
combustion engine, while in the
downstairs apartment the phone
keeps ringing.
He makes a peanut butter sandwich
and eats it.
After fiddling with the radio,
he turns it off.
He enumerates in his head
the exactest details of
face and voice of his first
dead friend, Fred Plunkett, while
down in the street the elementary
kids squeal home.
He thumbs through an old skin magazine.
After twenty-five pushups,
he rolls over on his back.
He thinks how much the ceiling
looks like an aerial photograph.
Not very much.
He falls asleep. When he wakes up,
it's dark outside. It could be
midnight.
After fiddling with the radio,
he turns it off.
With his forehead on the window
he thinks how much his mind

is like the Parthenon.
Not very much.

II. *Chiaroscuro with Pathetic Fallacy*

A man is lonely

The wind rattles the windows
of his apartment

The wind thrusts its tongue
deep in the mouth of the night

Oh! moans the night

A man is lonely
The night buries its head
deep in the shoulder of the wind

Oh! moans the wind

When a man is lonely
the wind is not the wind

The thrilled night arches toward the windows

Love Poem

There is a madman loose
in my one good eye.
He has a knife and he
wants to get out.
If you see me tonight,
don't look in my eyes.
One of them is ready
to hurt you. It would be
safer for you to ignore
my whole face. Cut off
my head in your mind, if
you know what's good for you.
In the rain forests the cannibals
are on fire. Soon
they will be darting down
the streets of your home town,
outside your door.

Little Song Without a Friend

The goalie
threw the game today

And the chef
spat in each entree

And the evangelist
the evangelist
the evangelist buttfucked the choirleader

And the beggar
broke his begging arm
when he tripped over
the policeman's blown off head

And I
wrote this little song today
And was ashamed of it immediately
And sleep was the hero of the day

The Night Nobody Said Anything

for Peter Handke

It is a sunny day.

Suddenly a cat slinks out of the house.

The house just stands there.

A pumpkin falls down.

It just falls down.
It represents falling down.

It is probably not necessary to mention that the pumpkin
is not the sun.

The cat does what it does.

Two people are not there, as if no one were watching.
They keep not being there.

The pause is noticeable, so slowly
that it is no longer a laughing matter.
   „ „ „ „   „   „   „
   „ „ „ „   „   „   „

No music is pleasant.

In the Italian spy film *The Chief Sends His Best Man*
(with Stewart Granger and Peter van Eyck, directed by
Sergio Sollima) there is also no music,
without the same consequences.

Can one gather from the manner of the cat
there soon will be music? Actually not.

The sun does what it does.
If it should decide to leave
no one should stop it
from doing so.

On the Future of Bridges

Bridges will strangle the air until
It confesses something terrible,

Something no one wants to know.
Then the bridges will let go.

Planning Ahead

I have always considered it bad policy to land on my head. I try my best to avoid doing so. The head is just not structured to bear the weight of the body, or to withstand more than an occasional semi-violent thump. The soles of the feet, on the other hand, manage this quite well. I have jumped from a few moving vehicles in my day, and let me tell you, the head is just a frightened onlooker in such instances.

Yet who sings of feet? Even Shakespeare, perhaps the greatest writer who ever lived, ignored them, so lost was he in the dizzying music of the head. The other morning, oh, I guess it was about three, I woke up with a shout. I was sweating and I felt very uncomfortable. Yes. I was having a nightmare. I was being pursued by human skeletons on motorcycles. I was trying to run, but they were getting closer and closer. I could see their fixed bloody grins, and their empty sockets stared lecherously at the flesh of my face. A thoroughly unpleasant dream. One I have quite often. I switched on the light, and went to get a glass of water. My rate of respiration was abnormally high, as if I had been engaging in violent exercise. In reality, of course, I had been sleeping. But it is a proven fact that psychic excitation often stimulates correlated physiological responses. As I was drinking, I had a thought which caused my heart to jump. I sat down immediately and began composing a letter to my darling, the sweetest most ethereal woman in the world, so far as I'm concerned. She was so far away she might as well have been in some foreign country. O my heart ached for her as I wrote! I inquired about her health, the weather, etc., merely as a way of dispelling my own fear. I told her all the news from home, the things I was writing, the plays I had seen, but I could not for long content myself with such trivial amenities. My pen began to pour forth the inevitable truth, the love I felt for her. "You are my only desire," I wrote, "I love you more than life / I am like a man dead until I am / holding your sweet face and touched / by the divinity of your breath." I sighed over the letter for an hour, finally sealing it in a white envelope to be mailed at daybreak. I climbed back in bed, but there was no more sleep for me. I lay there thinking about my sweetheart, recalling each tender caress we had shared.

The soul enters or leaves the body by one of two avenues: the nostrils and mouth (I consider these one), and the feet. Perhaps you didn't know it, but the feet are very erotic fellows. It is a medical fact that at the moment of sexual climax, the feet arch involuntarily and the toes curl. If you were to say this is the soul bowing to love, I would say, "Yes! O yes! That is possible!"

It is so easy to joke about feet. How is it that we who are so poker-faced about our heads can be so openly derisive about our feet? O yes, feet are often laughable, the way they look like prehistoric fish or crazy dragsters, and I enjoy a good laugh as much as the next guy, but I am angered by this constant belittling of feet. It has got to stop! I will continue to praise all feet. The feet of my love. The feet of our President. Your feet and mine.

Is it wrong to be sentimental about feet? I saw a footless man who cried all day because he missed his feet. I can certainly understand that.

63

Epitaph

Here lies Adam LeFevre:
ever a mad elf

Epitaph

Here lies Adam LeFevre:
ever a mad elf